Statman's Royal Ascot Special

Increase your chances of backing more winners at the World's most famous race meeting

Copyright © 2023 by Sean Trivass

All rights reserved. No part of this publication may be reproduced, distributed, or transmitted in any form or by any means, including photocopying, recording, or other electronic or mechanical methods, without the prior written permission of the publisher, except in the case of brief quotations embodied in critical reviews and certain other non-commercial uses permitted by copyright law.

Index

Royal Ascot Profiling – Why?	Page 1
A Little About The Author	Page 4
Royal Ascot Day One	Page 12
Royal Ascot Day Two	Page 26
Royal Ascot Day Three	Page 39
Royal Ascot Day Four	Page 53
Royal Ascot Day Five	Page 65
Testimonials	Page 78

The Royal Ascot meeting 2023 runs from Tuesday the 20th to Saturday 24th June, and for many racing fans (and social butterflys), this is the highlight of their calendar.

Five days of top-class competitive racing will no doubt see short-priced favourites succeed and fail, and if it is anything like previous years, those without sufficient weaponry (such as this) will struggle to make a profit, keeping the bookmakers rich and the punters poor. My objective is to make that competition balanced in your (our) favour, using past results to help to predict the likelier future winners, which I have done with great success before, both here and at other meetings.

You don't need any expertise to use this, just a general understanding of how to read the Racing Post (www.racingpost.com) where all the information is readily available in the free version (no need to subscribe), and I will talk you through one example of a different race (Royal Ascot runners are currently unknown), so you can practice what I preach.

Many of you may remember me from my "Statman" days, but even more of you will be new to the very concept. This is not a tipping book, there will be plenty of those available to help you part with your money but please ask yourself one question – if they know all the winners as some claim, why aren't they living on a yacht in the Caribbean – if only life was so simple eh?

~ 1 ~

This is slightly different and requires some work from you (shocking I know), but it has helped me and my followers to find plenty of winners at all prices over the years, and long may that continue.

The concept is sound – I have up to 26 years of statistics per race (some are newer, obviously) and each race is broken down in percentage order with the patterns of past winners. Ages, official ratings, position in the betting at the off, days since last run, and so on – but that is where my input ends.

By definition I cannot know all of those facts this far in advance (certainly not starting prices or even runners), so that is where you need to go to work. Using the statistics offered come race day, you should be able to cut a swathe through the large fields until you are left with a workable shortlist, though I should also add the "same" statistic may appear more than once in a list!

For example, if every winner had come home in the first 6 last time out that would be a high statistic – but I may also add 86% had come home in the first three – this is so you can run down the stats IN ORDER until you reach a number of horses left that YOU are happy with. You could then split your stakes on all the remaining runners using dutching software (https://www.oddschecker.com/betting-tools/dutching-calculator is my website of choice, but plenty of others

~ 2 ~

are available), or decide to favour one statistic over another to define your selection.

The choice is yours, but all I can tell you is that using the stats below would have found you the winner of the majority of races at Royal Ascot last year – though rarely as a pure one-off selection as mentioned earlier.

This is not opinion – this is historical fact and although some races will see a set of mixed results (alarm bells should start ringing), the majority fit a tried and trusted pattern – and long may that continue!

A Little About Your Author

No-one wants to read about me, and I don't need to tell you my life story either, but a little background may let you know where I come from, what I know – and why the following pages should prove worth reading if you want to increase your chances of making a profit from this meeting.

I have been involved in the sport for over 40 years, starting on the local paper with a weekly article where I was paid the grand sum of a fiver, in the days when I had to write in block capitals with a pen and paper – and cycle to the offices to stick it through their letterbox every Sunday – and no, those weren't the good old days!

Since then I have been to college where I got a Distinction in Quantitative Studies (or Stats to you and I), and for the last 20 years or so I have been a full-time freelance racing journalist writing for all sorts – including The Independent, BetDaq, Alan Brazil Racing Club, What Really Wins, Australian Thoroughbred News, The Daily Sport, Press Association, Post Racing, Worldofsport, Timeform, and numerous others in a rich and varied career.

Other books have been published so do have a look to see if you can find something that suits (search Trivass or

Statman on Amazon) – they have all been meticulously researched with one intention only – to make finding winners that little bit easier for us all.

Gambling Harm

As I write the Gambling review is out, and our sport is in the headlines. This book is not meant to encourage anyone to gamble, and I urge you all to think twice before placing any bets to make sure you can afford your hobby. For me, racing is exciting and fun – it's not about the gambling, it's about pitting my wits against those who compile the odds – and trying to find a way to beat the bookmakers – I can do that with small **affordable** bets and suggest you do the same. Do NOT let gambling overcome you, do NOT bet more than you can afford to lose – and DO make the most of all the tools available with your bookmaker such as time outs and deposit limits if needed. Please control your gambling (do not let it control you), and remember that help is available via the National Gambling Helpline (0808 8020 133), and online at Gamcare.org.uk with other services freely available.

Example – do note this is not a Royal Ascot race, but one picked from elsewhere as a one-off with its own set of criteria applicable to that race as a way to show how to use these statistics.

Example:

Unsurprisingly, I do not have an example to hand for Royal Ascot, so I will add in an example from elsewhere as an idea of how this can (and does) work.

Saturday 7th January 2023

Sandown 3.35pm - Unibet New And Improved Bet Builder Handicap Hurdle

This would be the equivalent list of appropriate stats (smaller, but stats lists vary by race throughout the year)

Remove horses from the final declaration list in the following order:

1 Any horse not in the first eight in the betting at the off (100%)
2 Any horse older than eight (100%)
3 Any horse younger than five (92%)
4 Any horse without a run this season (92%)
5 Any horse carrying more than 11 stone three (85%)
6 Any horse who completed and failed to finish in the first five last time out (85%)
7 Any horse rated below 121 (85%)
8 Any horse without a run in the last 60 days (85%)

Additional notes:

- Trainer Nicky Henderson has won this four times from nine runners (44%) and placed with another one
- Trainer Oliver Sherwood has won this with both his runners (100%)

This is the after-race card so you can see the betting at the off

3:35 Sandown
7 JAN 2023 ITV

2m (1m7f216y) Unibet New And Improved Bet Builder Handicap Hurdle (GBB Race) (Class 2) (4yo+ 0-145)

Going: 5
No. of hurdles:
EW Terms: 1/5

| Card | Pro Card | At-a-glance | Odds Comparison | Live | ? |

| Predictor | Newspaper Form | Settings | | | Select Bookmaker | Ladbrokes |

VIEW 1 OFFER FOR SANDOWN

NO. FORM	HORSE	AGE	WGT OR	JOCKEY ALLOWANCE / TRAINER RTF%	TS	RPR	ODDS
1 /23/6-	Band Of Outlaws > ⊙ 555 (232F)	8	12-0 142	J: Richie McLernon > T: [1] Ben Haslam >[27]	-	-	›22/1 ›25/1 ›22/1 ›25
2 0/74-1	Lightly Squeeze > t ⊙ 3 tips 47	9	11-8 136	J: Bryan Carver > T: Harry Fry >[50]	73	146	›6/1 ›13/2 ›6/1 ›1
3 5P6-P1	Poseidon > P ⊙ 30	9	11-7 135	J: Fergus Gillard >[3] T: [1] David Pipe >[25]	90	142	›66/1 ›50/1 ›66/1 ›50
4 7144-	Iceo > h ⊙ 7 tips 315	5	11-3 131	J: Harry Cobden > T: Paul Nicholls >[48]	125	141	›10/3 ›7/2 ›3/1 ›10
5 6100-9	Tiger Voice > ⊙ 254 (119F)	8	11-2 130	J: Robert Williams >[3] T: [1] Bernard Llewellyn >[25]	-	143	›33/1 ›40/1 ›33/1 ›40
6 1-12	Djelo > ⊙ 2 tips 38	5	11-1 129	J: Charlie Deutsch > T: Venetia Williams >[37]	118	143	›13/8 ›7/4 ›13/8 ›1
7 P/7/0-	Palladium > ⊙ 559 (529F)	7	10-12 126	J: Nico de Boinville > T: [1] Polly Gundry >	-	-	›18/1 ›22/1 ›25/1 ›22
8 222-53	Hardy Du Seuil > ⊙ 1 tip 56	6	10-10 124	J: Gavin Sheehan > T: Jamie Snowden >[36]	132	145	›5/1 ›9/2 ›5/1 ›9
9 2118-2	Dr T J Eckleburg > ⊙ 41	5	10-7 121	J: Aidan Coleman > T: Olly Murphy >[32]	119	142	›11/1 ›10/1 ›11/1 ›10
11 32142-	Imphal > P ⊙ 1 tip 266	9	10-3 117	J: Caoilin Quinn >[5] T: Gary Moore >[60]	137	145	›22/1 ›20/1 ›22/1 ›2
NR 116-F6	In The Air > ⊙ 1 tip 50	5	10-6 120	J: T: Gary Moore >	59	140	

Show all racecards for this meeting on one page >

BETTING FORECAST 3/1 Lightly Squeeze, 7/2 Djelo, 11/2 Iceo, 6/1 In The Air, 7/1 Hardy Du Seuil, 8/1 Dr T J Eckleburg, 14/1 Imphal, 20/1 Palladium, Poseidon, 40/1 Band Of Outlaws, Tiger Voice.

~ 9 ~

So, running through the list above (in order) for our example...

1. Remove/put a line though Poseidon and Tiger Voice
2. Remove/put a line Lightly Squeeze, Poseidon, and Imphal
3. No horses aged under five to remove
4. Remove/put a line Band Of Outlaws, Iceo, Palladium, and Imphal
5. Remove/put a line Band Of Outlaws, Light Squeeze, and Poseidon
6. Remove/put a line Band Of Outlaws, Tiger Voice, and Palladium
7. Remove/put a line Imphal
8. Remove/put a line Band Of Outlaws, Iceo, Tiger Voice, Palladium, and Imphal

Doing all of the above (I am aware many horses were removed numerous times but this is an example), we are left with a shortlist of

Djelo
Hardy Du Seuil
Dr T J Eckleburg

If you dutched all three using dutching software you would make a profit of over 57% BUT, if you are greedy (like me), then I looked at three other factors – Anything of note from the Additional Notes (not in this case), RTF

(Running To Form) figure (very similar on this occasion), and whether they are being asked to do anything they haven't proved capable of before. Djelo raced off a mark of 129 (highest winning mark 114) Hard Du Seuil 124 (highest winning mark 129), and Dt T J Eckleburg 121 (highest winning mark 115), so for me, all roads lead to the chances of **Hardi Du Seuil**, though being the coward I am, all horses priced at 4/1 or above are each way bets to me.

Result: Hard Du Seuil Won 4/1 by three lengths, Iceo 2nd 3/1, Djelo 3rd 15/8f, Dr T J Eckleburg 4th 12/1. The winner clearly pointed to via the stats as well as the third and the fourth.

All you need to do now is the same for every race at Royal Ascot – the original (100% only) list will trap more winners than not, the choice is yours how far down the rest of the list you go.

Day One
Tuesday 20th June 2023 (race times and titles subject to change)

*NOTE for all races -any weight referred to is the allocated weight and does not take into account any jockey claims or overweights)

Race One: The Queen Anne Stakes (Group One) 2.30pm

Our first race, and 26 years of statistics to work with. As with all races, head to your website or publication of choice (I use www.racingpost.com) and work down the final declarations as follows. It is unlikely any one horse will fit all the criteria so stop when you reach the number of remaining horses that you are happy to deal with (or Dutch as you see fit). This applies to all races and will not be repeated (you will be pleased to know). Please note – when it comes to official ratings this only applies to horses with an official rating – those without should NOT be removed using this criteria unless it is specifically stated otherwise.

DO NOTE: 100% IS THE "GOLD STANDARD", BUT MAY LEAVE TOO MANY HORSES ON YOUR SHORT LIST – ANY

FIGURES LOWER THAN 100% SHOULD <u>THEN BE USED AS NECESSARY</u> TO CARRY ON THOUGH THE REMAINING RUNNERS AND REDUCE THE QUALIFIERS FURTHER IF YOU WISH – DITTO THE "ADDITIONAL NOTES" THAT HAVE BEEN ADDED TO ASSIST YOU IN YOUR SEARCH FOR THE WINNER, WHICH ARE <u>NOT</u> PART OF THE STATISTICAL ANALYSIS.

Remove horses from the final declaration list in the following order:

1 Any horse priced larger than 33/1 at the off (100%)
2 Any three-year-old (100%)
3 Any horse with more than two runs this season (100%)
4 Any horse older than six (100%)
5 Any horse outside the first eight in the betting (96%)
6 Any horse older than five (96%)
7 Any horse drawn higher than 12 (96%)
8 Any horse with an official rating lower than 112 (95%)
9 Any horse priced larger than 20/1 at the off (92%)
10 Any horse priced larger than 12/1 at the off (88%)

<u>Additional notes:</u>

- Fourteen horses won this after racing in the Lockinge Stakes at Newbury on their last start
- Two horses won here on their first start since running in the Juddmonte Stakes at York on their previous run.

- Trainer Aidan O'Brien has won this four times from 25 runners (16%) and placed with a further five (36% total)
- Trainer Sir Michael Stoute has won this three times from 16 attempts (19%) and placed with a further four (44% total)
- Trainer Saeed Bin Suroor has won this six times from 22 runners (27%) and placed with one other (32% total)
- Jockey Frankie Dettori has won this six times from 16 rides (38%) and placed with one other (44% total)

Race Two: The Coventry Stakes (Group Two) 3.05pm

Remove horses from the final declaration list in the following order:

1 Any horse having their first ever run (100%)
2 Any horse who finished outside the first seven on their previous start (100%)
3 Any horse who has had a race in the last seven days (100%)
4 Any horse priced larger than 20/1 at the off (96%)
5 Any horse with more than two runs this season (96%)
6 Any horse who finished outside the first five on their previous start (96%)
7 Any horse who failed to win last time out (92%)
8 Any horse outside of the first nine in the betting at the off (92%)

Additional notes:

- Four horses came here after last running the in the Marble Hill Stakes at The Curragh and were successful
- Trainer John Gosden (now John and Thady Gosden) has won this twice from 12 runners (17%) and placed with two others (33% total)
- Trainer Aidan O'Brien has won this nine times from 40 runners (23%) and placed with a further six (38% total)

~ 15 ~

- Jockey Frankie Dettori has won this twice from 21 rides (10%) and placed on a further six occasions (38% total)
- Jockey Ryan Moore has won this three times from 17 mounts (18%) and placed on four other rides (41% total)
- Jockey Jamie Spencer has won this twice from 14 rides (14%) and placed on two others (29% total)

Race Three: The King's Stand Stakes (Group One) 3.40pm

Remove horses from the final declaration list in the following order:

1 Any horse priced bigger than 33/1 at the off (100%)
2 Any horse drawn higher than 18 (100%)
3 Any horse who ran in the last seven days (100%)
4 Any horse who finished outside of the first seven last time out (100%)
5 Any horse rated lower than 102 (100%)
6 Any horse aged nine or older (100%)
7 Any horse who finished outside of the first five last time out (96%)
8 Any horse aged older than seven (96%)
9 Any horse rated less than 106 (96%)
10 Any horse who raced in the last 15 days (96%)
11 Any horse with more than three runs this season (96%)
12 Any horse rated less than 111 (92%)

Additional notes:

- Seven horses came here and won after last running in the Temple Stakes at Haydock
- Two horses came here and won after last running in the Nunthorpe Stakes at York
- Trainer Charlie Appleby has won this twice from six runners (33%)

- Trainer Robert Cowell has won this twice from 12 runners (17%) and placed with one other (25% total)
- Trainer Ed Lynam has win this twice from five runners (40%) and placed with on other (60% total)
- Jockey Jim Crowley has won this twice from 10 rides (20%) and placed on two others (40% total)
- Jockey Olivier Peslier has won this twice from 10 mounts (20%)

Race Four: The St James's Palace Stakes (Group One) 4.20pm

Remove horses from the final declaration list in the following order:

1 Any horse priced bigger than 10/1 at the off (100%)
2 Any horse not in the first six in the betting at the off (100%)
3 Any horse who ran in the last seven days (100%)
4 Any horse with more than three runs this season (100%)
5 Any horse rated lower than 109 (100%)
6 Any horse drawn higher than 11 (96%)
7 Any horse not in the first five in the betting at the off (96%)
8 Any horse who failed to finish in the first six last time out (92%)
9 Any horse not in the first four in the betting (92%)

Additional notes:

- 13 horses have come here and won after running in the Irish 2000 Guineas on their last start
- Four horses have come here and been successful after last running in the English 2000 Guineas
- Trainer Jim Bolger has won this twice from six attempts (33%)

- Trainer John Gosden (now John and Thady Gosden) has won this three times from 19 attempts (16%) and placed with five others (42% total)
- Trainer Aidan O'Brien has won this race eight times from 55 runners (15%) and placed with a further 13 (38% total)
- Jockey Frankie Dettori has ridden the winner four times from 20 rides (20%) and placed on three others (35% total)
- Jockey James Doyle has won this twice from eight rides (25%)
- Jockey Ryan Moore has won this twice from 15 rides (13%) and placed on another six (53% total)

Race Five: The Ascot Stakes 5.00pm

Remove horses from the final declaration list in the following order:

1 Any horse who failed to come home in the first 11 last time out (100%)
2 Any horse aged older than nine (100%)
3 Any horse who hasn't had a run in the last 120 days (100%)
4 Any horse priced bigger than 40/1 at the off (96%)
5 Any horse aged older than eight (96%)
6 Any horse who hasn't had a run in the last 90 days (96%)
7 Any horse with more than three runs this season (92%)
8 Any horse priced bigger than 20/1 at the off (88%)
9 Any horse who failed to finish in the first eight last time out (88%)

Additional notes:

- Four horses came here after running in the Chester Cup on their last outing and won
- Two horses have come here and won after having their last outing in the two-mile Class Two handicap at Haydock in May
- Two horses have come here and won after having their last outing in the two and a half mile handicap hurdle at the Punchestown Festival

~ 21 ~

- Trainer A J Martin has won this twice from seven attempts (29%) and placed with three others (71% total)
- Trainer W P Mullins has won this contest four times from 19 runners (21%) and placed with six others (53% total)
- Trainer Ian Williams has won this twice from 13 starts (15%) and placed with one other (23%)
- Jockey Ryan Moore has won this three times from 19 mounts (16%) and placed another six times (47% total)

Race Six: The Wolferton Stakes (Listed) 5.35pm

Remove horses from the final declaration list in the following order (note – only 21 runnings of this race):

1 Any horse priced larger than 25/1 at the off (100%)
2 Any horse who ran in the last seven days (100%)
3 Any horse with more than three runs this season (100%)
4 Any horse drawn higher than 15 (100%)
5 Any horse without a run in the last 365 days (100%)
6 Any horse who failed to finish in the first seven last time out (95%)
7 Any horse rated higher than 112 (95%)
8 Any horse aged older than six (90%)

Additional notes:

- Two horses came here after running in the 1m 2.5f handicap at York in May and won here
- Two horses came here after running in the Hambleton Stakes at York in May and won here
- Trainer John Gosden (now John and Thady Gosden) has won this race four times from 16 runners (25%) and placed with four others (50% total)
- Trainer Sir Michael Stoute has win this twice from 18 runners (11%) and placed with seven others (50% total)

- Jockey William Buick has won this twice from 12 rides (17%) and placed with one other (25% total)
- Jockey Ryan Moore has won this twice from 17 mounts (12%) and placed on five others (41% total)
- Jockey Danny Tudhope has won this twice from four rides (50%)

Race Seven: The Copper Horse Stakes 6.10pm

With just the three runnings of this race so far it does not qualify for any sensible statistical analysis.

Day Two
Wednesday 21st June 2023 (race times and titles subject to change)

Race One: The Queen Mary Stakes (Group Two) 2.30pm

Re**move** horses from the final declaration list in the following order:

1 Any horse priced larger than 25/1 at the off (100%)
2 Any horse who failed to finish in the first three last time out (if they have raced before) (100%)
3 Any horse who has raced within the last seven days (100%)
4 Any horse (who has raced before) who hasn't had a run in the last 60 days ()100%)
5 Any horse priced shorter than 13/8 at the off (100%)
6 Any horse who failed to finish in the first two last time out (96%)
7 Any horse with more than three runs this season (92%)

Additional notes:

- Four winners have come here after last running in the Marygate Fillies Stakes at York in May and went on to win this

- Three horses had their previous run in the National Stakes at Sandown in May before winning here
- Two horses came here after competing in the Fillies Sprint Stakes at Naas in May and were successful
- Trainer Mick Channon (now Jack Channon) has won this three times from seventeen runners (18%) and placed with another two (29% total)
- Trainer Mark Johnston (now Charlie Johnston) has won this twice from 14 runners (14%)
- Trainer Wesley Ward has won this four times from 15 runners (27%) and placed with another four (53% total)
- Jockey Frankie Dettori has won this four times from 21 rides (19%) and placed on four other occasions (38% total)

Race Two: The Kensington Palace Stakes 3.05pm

This is a new race added to the card as recently as 20221 and as such, we have no useful statistics to go to war with.

Race Three: The Duke Of Cambridge Stakes (Group Two) 3.40pm

Remove horses from the final declaration list in the following order (note 19 runnings of this particular race):

1 Any horse priced larger than 25/1 at the off (100%)
2 Any horse drawn higher than 12 (100%)
3 Any horse making their debut (100%)
4 Any horse rated lower than 103 (100%)
5 Any horse who ran in the last seven days (100%)
6 Any horse who failed to finish in the first five last time out (100%)
7 Any horse who failed to finish in the first four last time out (95%)
8 Any horse not in the first six in the betting (95%)
9 Any horse with more than two previous runs this season (95%)

Additional notes:

- Four horses arrived here after running in the Dahlia Stakes at Newmarket and went on to win
- Four horses arrived here after running in the Princess Margaret Stakes at Epsom and went on to win
- Two horses arrived here after running in the Lanwades Stud Stakes at The Curragh and went on to win
- Two horses arrived here after running in the Chartwell Fillies Stakes at Lingfield and went on to win
- Two horses arrived here after running in the Sun Chariot Stakes at Newmarket in October and went on to win
- Trainer James Fanshawe has won this twice from nine runners (22%) and placed with four others (67% total)
- Trainer John Gosden (now John and Thady Gosden) has won this four times from eight runners (50%) and placed with one other (63%)
- Trainer Sir Michael Stoute has won this four times from 20 attempts (20%) and placed a further seven tines (55% total)
- Jockey William Buick has ridden the winner three times from 12 rides (25%)and placed on one more (33% total)
- Jockey Wayne Lordan has won this twice from two rides (100%)

- Jockey Ryan Moore has ridden the winner twice from 15 rides (13%) and placed four times (40% total)

Race Four: The Prince Of Wales's Stakes (Group One) 4.20pm

Remove horses from the final declaration list in the following order:

1 Any horse larger than 20/1 at the off (100%)
2 Any horse who failed to finish in the first six last time out (100%)
3 Any three-year-old (100%)
4 Any horse outside the first seven in the betting (100%)
5 Any horse with an official rating of less than 109 (100%)
6 Any horse older than six (100%)
7 Any horse outside the first six on the betting (96%)
8 Any horse from a stall higher than nine (96%)
9 Any horse that failed to finish in the first four last time out (96%)
10 Any horse with a rating of less than 112 (96%)
11 Any horse older than five (96%)
12 Any horse with more than two runs this season (96%)
13 Any horse with a rating of less than 117 (92%)
14 Any horse outside the first four in the betting (92%)

Additional notes:

- Six horses went on to win this after last running in the Tattersalls Gold Cup at The Curragh

~ 31 ~

- Three horses arrived here after last racing in the Brigadier Gerard Stakes at Sandown and went on to win
- Trainer Andre Fabre has had two winners here from five runners (40%) and has placed with a further two (80% total)
- Trainer John Gosden (now John and Thady Gosden) has won this twice from 18 attempts (11%) and placed with another six (44% total)
- Trainer Aidan O'Brien has won this four times from 24 runners (17%) and placed with seven others (44% total)
- Trainer Sir Michael Stoute has won this twice from 21 runners (10%) and placed with a further seven (44% total)
- Trainer Saeed Bin Suroor has won this four times from 20 runners (20%) and placed with five more (45% total)
- Jockey Frankie Dettori has won this four times from 22 rides (18%) and placed on a further eight occasions (55% total)
- Jockey James Doyle has won this three times from five rides (60%)
- Jockey Ryan Moore has won this twice from 15 mounts (13%) and placed on six others (53% total)
- Jockey Oliver Peslier has won this twice from eight rides (25%) and placed with one other (38% total)

Race Five: The Royal Hunt Cup 5.00pm

Remove horses from the final declaration list in the following order:

1 Any horse priced larger than 33/1 at the off (100%) (100%)

2 Any horse coming out of the one or two stall (100%)

3 Any horse coming out of stalls 18 to 20 (100%)

4 Any horse coming out of stalls 29-32 (100%)

5 Any three-year-old (100%)

6 Any horse who raced within in the last seven days (100%)

7 Any horse older than seven (100%)

8 Any horse with more than four runs this season (100%)

9 Any horse rated higher than 105 (100%)

10 Any horse carrying more than nine stone five (100%)

11 Any horse older than six (96%)

12 Any horse rated lower than 88 (96%)

13 Any horse rated lower than 91 (92%)

14 Any horse rated higher than 103 (92%)

15 Any horse older than five (88%)

16 Any horse not in the first 11 in the betting at the off (88%)

Additional Notes:

- Three horses raced here after having their previous start in the Victoria Cup here at Ascot in May and won

- Two horses came here after competing in the Hambleton Stakes at York and went on to win
- Two horses won this after having their latest start the previous year in the Cambridgeshire at Newmarket
- Two horses ran in the one mile handicap at Sandown in May and were then successful here
- Trainer James Fanshawe has won this twice from his 11 attempts (18%) and placed with a further four (55% total)
- Trainer John Gosden (now John and Thady Gosden) has won this twice from 23 runners (9%) and placed with another four (26% total)
- Trainer Charlie Hills has won this on two occasions from eight tries (25%) and placed with two others (50% total)
- Trainer Saeed Bin Suroor has a record of two from 13 (15%) with another two hitting the frame (31% total)
- Jockey Frankie Dettori has won this twice from 21 attempts (10%) and placed on three others (24% total)
- Jockey James Doyle has won this twice from 10 rides (20%) and placed on two others (40% total)

Race Six: The Queen's Vase (Group Two) 5.35pm

Remove horses from the final declaration list in the following order:

1 Any horse priced larger than 33/1 at the off (100%)
2 Any horse who failed to finish in the first 11 last time out (100%)
3 Any horse who raced in the last seven days (100%)
4 Any horse coming out of stall 13 or higher (100%)
5 Any horse with an official rating lower than 85 (100%)
6 Any horse priced larger than 11/1 (96%)
7 Any horse who failed to finish in the first nine last time out (96%)
8 Any horse outside the first six in the betting at the off (96%)
9 Any horse who failed to finish in the first four last time out (92%)
10 Any horse with an official rating lower than 94 (92%)
11 Any horse without a race in the last 90 days (92%)

Additional Notes:

- Four horses won this after having their previous start in the Lingfield Derby Trial
- Two horses came here after racing in the Epsom Derby on their previous start and were successful

- Trainer Mark Johnston (now Charlie Johnston) has won this seven times from 32 runners (22%) and placed with a further two (28% total)
- Trainer Aidan O'Brien has won this seven times from 34 attempts (21%) and placed with another eight (44% total)
- Trainer Sir Michael Stoute has run 12 horses here and succeeded with four of them (33%), placing with one other (42% total)
- Trainer Saeed Bin Suroor has won this twice from 10 runners (20%) and placed with two more (40% total)
- Jockey Frankie Dettori has won this twice from 16 rides (13%) and placed with four more (38% total)
- Jockey Ryan Moore has won this five times from 16 rides (31%) and placed on four others (56% total)

Race Seven: The Windsor Castle Stakes (Listed) 6.10pm

Remove horses from the final declaration list in the following order:

1 Any horse who failed to finish in the first six last time out (100%)
2 Any horse who has raced before and has not had a run in the last 60 days (100%)
3 Any horse with more than three runs this season (100%)
4 Any horse priced larger than 33/1 at the off (96%)
5 Any horse who failed to finish in the first four last time out (92%)
6 Any horse not in the first 10 in the betting at the off (88%)

Additional Notes:

- Two horses came here and won after last racing in the National Stakes at Sandown in May
- Two horses came here and won after last racing in the Marble Hill Stakes at The Curragh in May
- Trainer Mick Channon (now Jack Channon) has won this twice from 18 attempts (11%) and placed with four others (33% total)
- Trainer Aidan O'Brien has won this three times from 20 attempts (15%) and placed with two others (25% total)

- Trainer Jamie Osborne has won this twice from four runners (50%)
- Trainer Wesley Ward has won this twice from 17 attempts (12%)
- Jockey Ryan Moore has won this three times from 16 mounts (19%) and placed with one other (25% total)

Day Three
Thursday 22nd June 2023 (race times and titles subject to change)

Race One: The Norfolk Stakes (Group Two) 2.30pm

Remove horses from the final declaration list in the following order:

1 Any horse who finished outside the top six on their last start (100%)
2 Any horse with more than four runs (100%)
3 Any horse who has had a race in the last seven days (100%)
4 Any horse priced larger than 33/1 at the off (96%)
5 Any horse who finished outside the front four on their last start (96%)
6 Any horse not making their debut who has not raced in the last 60 days (96%)
7 Any horse drawn higher than 12 (96%)
8 Any horse outside the front six in the betting at the off (92%)
9 Any horse priced larger than 16/1 at the off (92%)
10 Any horse who finished outside the front three on their last start (92%)

Additional Notes:

- Three horses came here after running in the Beverley Two-Year-Old Trophy and win
- Two horses came here after running in the Woodcote Stakes at Epsom and were successful
- Trainer Peter Chapple-Hyam has won this twice from six runners (33%) and placed with one other (50% total)
- Trainer Richard Fahey has run nine here and won this twice (22%) with another placed (33% total)
- Trainer William Haggas has won this twice from seven starters (29%)
- Trainer Aidan O'Brien has won this three times from 23 runners (13%) and placed with six others (39% total)
- Trainer Wesley Ward has won this twice from 10 attempts (20%) and placed with one other (30% total)
- Jockey Frankie Dettori has won this three times from 16 rides (19%) and placed on five other occasions (50% total)
- Jockey Paul Hanagan has won this twice from seven mounts (29%) and placed with one other (43% total)
- Jockey Ryan Moore has won this twice from eighteen attempts (11%) and placed on four others (33% total)

- Jockey Joel Rosario has won this twice from two rides (100%)

Race Two: The King George V Stakes 3.05pm

Remove horses from the final declaration list in the following order:

1 Any horse who failed to finish in the first nine last time out (100%)
2 Any horse rated below 80 (100%)
3 Any horse rated above 99 (100%)
4 Any horse without a run in the last 60 days (100%)
5 Any horse priced larger than 22/1 at the off (96%)
6 Any horse outside the first 12 in the betting at the off (96%)
7 Any horse who failed to finish in the first three last time out (96%)
8 Any horse who raced in the last seven days (96%)
9 Any horse with more than four runs this season (96%)
10 Any horse outside the first 10 in the betting (92%)

Additional Notes:

- Two horses came here after running in the Class Three mile and a quarter handicap at Sandown at the end of May
- Two horses came here and won after having their last start in the mile and a quarter handicap at the Epsom Derby meeting
- Trainer Charlie Appleby has won this twice from 12 starters (17%) and placed with a further three (42% total)

~ 42 ~

- Trainer Mark Johnston (now Charlie Johnston) has won this five times from 64 attempts (8%) and placed with a further seven (19% total)
- Trainer Sir Michael Stoute has won this four times from 30 runners (13%) and placed with a further seven (37% total)
- Jockey William Buick has won this twice from 11 rides (18%) and placed on five others (64% total)

Race Three: The Ribblesdale Stakes (Group Two) 3.40pm

Remove horses from the final declaration list in the following order:

1 Any horse priced at larger than 25/1 at the off (100%)
2 Any horse outside the first nine in the betting at the off (100%)
3 Any horse rated lower than 88 (100%)
4 Any horse rated higher than 110 (100%)
5 Any horse with more than three runs this season (96%)
6 Any horse who failed to finish in the first seven last time out (88%)

Additional Notes:

- Seven horses came here after having their last start in the Epsom Oaks and were successful
- Two horses came here after having the last start in the Newmarket 1000 Guineas and were successful
- Trainer Aidan O'Brien has raced 29 horses here and won with three of them (10%), placing with a further six (31% total)
- Trainer Saeed Bin Suroor has won this five times from 11 attempts (45%) and placed with two others (64% total)
- Trainer Dermot Weld has won this twice from two runners (100%)

- Jockey Frankie Dettori has won this seven times from 20 mounts (35%) and placed on two others (45% total)
- Jockey Ryan Moore has won this three times from 17 rides (18%) and placed on four others (41% total)

Race Four: The Gold Cup (Group One) 4.20pm

Remove horses from the final declaration list in the following order:

1 Any horse priced larger than 20/1 at the off (100%)
2 Any horse drawn higher than 14 (100%)
3 Any horse who failed to finish in the first nine last time out (100%)
4 Any horse older than eight (100%)
5 Any horse who ran in the last seven days (100%)
6 Any horse having their first run on the Flat (100%)
7 Any horse without a run in the Flat in the last 365 days (100%)
8 Any horse rated below 107 (100%)
9 Any horse with more than three runs this season (96%)
10 Any horse older than seven (96%)
11 Any horse rated below 111 (96%)
12 Any horse older than six (92%)
13 Any horse with more than two runs this season (92%)
14 Any horse rated below 115 (88%)

Additional Notes:

- Eight horses came here after running in the Henry II Stakes at Sandown last time out and were successful
- Five horses went on to win this after running in the Saval Beg Stakes at Leopardstown in May

- Three horses came here after running in the Yorkshire Cup at York in May and were successful
- Three horses came here after running in the Vintage Crop Stakes at Navan in May and were successful
- Two horses came here after running in the Sagaro Stakes At Ascot and were successful
- Trainer John Gosden (now John and Thady Gosden) has won this three times from 13 runners (23%) and placed with two others (38% total)
- Trainer Mark Johnston (now Charlie Johnston) has had 18 runners in this and won with three of them (17%), placing with a further four (39% total)
- Trainer Aidan O'Brien has won this eight times from his 23 attempts (35%) and placed with three others (48% total)
- Trainer Saeed Bin Suroor has won this four times from 32 runners (13%) and placed with three others (22% total)
- Jockey Frankie Dettori has won this six times from 23 attempts (26%) and placed a further three times (39% total)
- Jockey Ryan Moore has won this three times from 17 rides (18%) and placed on a further four (41% total)

Race Five: The Britannia Stakes 5.00pm

Remove horses from the final declaration list in the following order:

1 Any horse priced larger than 33/1 at the off (100%)
2 Any horse rated lower than 83 (100%)
3 Any horse who last ran within the last seven days (100%)
4 Any horse with more than four previous runs this season (100%)
5 Any horse who failed to come home in the first five on their last start (96%)
6 Any horse rated lower than 85 (96%)
7 Any horse without a run in the last 90 days (96%)
8 Any horse with more than three runs this season (96%)
9 Any horse not in the first 14 in the betting at the off (96%)
10 Any horse making their seasonal debut (96%)
11 Any horse rated lower than 87 (92%)

Additional Notes:

- Three horses arrive here after running in the Haydock Silver Bowl and were successful
- Two horses won this after having their prior start in the one-mile Class Three handicap at Newmarket in May

- Two horses won this after having their prior start in the seven-and-a-half-furlong Class Two handicap at Chester at the May Festival
- Trainers Roger and Harry Charlton have won this twice from nine attempts (22%)
- Trainer John Gosden (now John and Thady Gosden) has won this three times from 43 runners (7%) and placed with seven others (23% total)
- Jockey Ryan Moore has won this race three times from 19 tries (16%) and placed on five others (42% total)
- Jockey Frannie Norton has won this twice from 12 rides (17%)
- Jockey Jamie Spencer has won this four times from 19 rides (21%) and placed on four others (48% total)

Race Six: The Hampton Court Stakes (Group Three) 5.35pm

Remove horses from the final declaration list in the following order:

1 Any horse priced larger than 33/1 at the off (100%)
2 Any horse coming out of a stall higher than 12 (100%)
3 Any horse rated lower than 90 (100%)
4 Any horse who ran in the last seven days (100%)
5 Any horse rated higher than 113 (100%)
6 Any horse priced larger than 20/1 at the off (96%)
7 Any horse who failed to finish in the first nine last time out (96%)
8 Any horse priced shorter than 13/8 at the off (96%)
9 Any horse rated lower than 93 (96%)
10 Any horse rated higher than 111 (96%)
11 Any horse who failed to finish in the first six last time out (92%)

Additional Notes:

- Three horses came here after running in the Epsom Derby on their last start and walked away the winner
- Two horses last ran in the London Gold Cup at Newbury before then winning here
- Two horses last ran in the Dante Stakes at York in May before then winning here

- Two horses last ran in the Newmarket Stakes in early May before then winning here
- Trainer John Gosden (now John and Thady Gosden) has had 15 runners here for two winners (13%) with two others placing (27% total)
- Trainer William Haggas has won this twice from six runners (33%) and placed with one other (50% total)
- Trainer Aidan O'Brien has won this four times from 23 runners (17%) and placed with four others (35% total)
- Trainer Sir Michael Stoute has won this three times from 23 attempts (13%) and placed with four more (30% total)
- Jockey William Buick has ridden the winner twice from eight attempts (25%)
- Jockey Frankie Dettori has ridden 20 times in this race and won on three of them (15%) with two others placing (25%)
- Jockey Ryan Moore has won this four times from 17 mounts (24%) and placed on four others (47% total)

Race Seven: The Buckingham Palace Stakes 6.10pm (note – only 16 runnings of this particular contest):

<u>Remove</u> horses from the final declaration list in the following order:

1 Any horse priced larger than 33/1 at the off (100%)
2 Any horse priced shorter than 8/1 at the off (100%)
3 Any horse aged older than eight (100%)
4 Any horse without a run in the last 365 days (100%)
5 Any horse rated higher than 103 (100%)
6 Any horse rated lower than 80 (100%)
7 Any three-year-old (94%)
8 Any horse without a run in the last 60 days (94%)
9 Any horse rated higher than 101 (94%)
10 Any horse with more than four runs this season (94%)
11 Any horse rated lower than 87 (94%)
12 Any horse older than seven (94%)
13 Any horse older than six (88%)
14 Any horse who failed to finish in the first eight last time out (88%)

Additional Notes:

- Two winners of this race had their previous start in the Victoria Cup here at Ascot in May
- Jockey Adam Kirby has won this twice from eight rides (25%)

Day Four
Friday 23rd June 2023 (race times and titles subject to change)

Race One: The Albany Stakes (Group Three) 2.30pm (note: 21 runnings of this particular race)

Remove horses from the final declaration list in the following order:

1 Any horse who failed to finish in the first four last time out (100%)
2 Any horse who ran in the last seven days (100%)
3 Any horse who has raced before but is without a run in the last 60 days (100%)
4 Any horse with more than two runs (100%)
5 Any horse who finished second last time out (100%)
6 Any horse priced larger than 20/1 at the off (92%)
7 Any horse drawn higher than 17 (92%)
8 Any horse who failed to finish in the first three last time out (92%)
9 Any horse outside the first nine in the market at the off (92%)

Additional Notes:

- Two horses have arrived here after running in the Fillies' Sprint Stakes at Naas and been successful
- Trainer Mick Channon (now Jack Channon) has won this three times from 17 runners (18%) and placed with two others (29% total)
- Trainer Aidan O'Brien has won this twice from 18 runners (11%) and placed with a further five (39% total)
- Trainer Roger Varian has won this with tow of his six runners (33%) and placed with one other (50% total)
- Jockey Jamie Spencer has won this four times from 11 rides (36%) and placed on three others (64% total)

Race Two: The Commonwealth Cup (Group One) 3.05pm (note only eight runnings so beware!)

Remove horses from the final declaration list in the following order:

1 Any horse priced larger than 12/1 at the off (100%)
2 Any horse drawn higher than 14 (100%)
3 Any horse rated lower than 107 (100%)
4 Any horse who raced in the last 15 days (100%)
5 Any horse with more than two starts this season (100%)
6 Any horse drawn higher than 10 (88%)
7 Any horse who finished outside the first seven on their last start (88%)
8 Any horse rated lower than 113 (88%)
9 Any horse who raced in the last 30 days (88%)
10 Any horse who finished outside of the first four last time out (75%)

Additional Notes:

- Two horses arrived here after running in the Newmarket 2000 Guineas and were successful
- Jockey Frankie Dettori has won this race twice from five rides (40%) and placed on two others (80% total)

Race Three: The Duke Of Edinburgh Stakes 3.40pm

Remove horses from the final declaration list in the following order:

1 Any horse priced at bigger than 33/1 at the off (100%)
2 Any horse that failed to finish in the first 12 home last time out (100%)
3 Any horse without a previous run (100%)
4 Any horde older than seven (100%)
5 Any horse rated higher than 104 (100%)
6 Any horse rated lower than 71 (100%)
7 Any horse priced at larger than 25/1 at the off (96%)
8 Any horse older than five (96%)
9 Any horse without a run in the last 365 days (96%)
10 Any three-year-old (96%)
11 Any horse rated lower than 80 (96%)
12 Any horse who has raced in the last seven days (96%)
13 Any horse with more than six runs this season (96%)
14 Any horse who failed to finish in the first eight last time out (92%)
15 Any horse rated lower than 89 (92%)

Additional Notes:

- Four horses came here after running in the mile and a half handicap at the Newmarket Guineas Festival and picked up first prize

- Four horses came here after running in the mile and a half handicap at the Epsom Derby Festival and were successful
- Two horses came here after running in the Jorvik Stakes at York in May and won this
- Trainer Mark Johnston (now Charlie Johnston) has won this four times from 30 runners (13%) and placed with another 5 (30% total)
- Trainer Hughie Morrison has won this four times from nine runners (44%) and placed with one other (56% total)
- Trainer Sir Michael Stoute has won this five times from 18 runners (28%) and placed with five others (56% total)
- Jockey William Buick has won this twice from 11 rides (18%) and placed on two others (36% total)
- Jockey Ryan Moore has won this four times from 16 mounts (25%) and placed on two more (38% total)

Race Four: The Coronation Stakes (Group One) 4.20pm

Remove horses from the final declaration list in the following order:

1 Any horse priced larger than 25/1 at the off (100%)
2 Any horse who ran in the last seven days (100%)
3 Any horse with more than four runs this season (100%)
4 Any horse rated lower than 100 (100%)
5 Any horse drawn higher than 12 (96%)
6 Any horse with more than three runs this season (96%)
7 Any horse priced larger than 20/1 at the off (96%)
8 Any horse rated lower than 104 (96%)
9 Any horse who ran in the last 15 days (96%)
10 Any horse who failed to finish in the first seven last time out (92%)
11 Any horse with more than two runs this season (92%)
12 Any horse rated lower than 108 (92%)

Additional Notes:

- Nine horses came here after running in the Newmarket 1000 Guineas and were successful
- Six horses won this after having their previous start in the Irish 1000 Guineas
- Trainer John Gosden (now John and Thady Gosden) has trained three winners from 23 attempts (13%) and placed with seven others (43% total)

- Trainers Mrs John Harrington has won this twice from three attempts (67%) and placed with her other runner (100% total)
- Trainer Aidan O'Brien has won this three times from 35 runners (9%) and placed with six others (26% total)
- Trainer Jean-Claude Rouget has won this twice from five attempts (40%) and placed with one more (60% total)
- Trainer Sir Michael Stoute has won this twice from 14 runners (14%) and placed with three others (36% total)
- Jockey Frankie Dettori has won this twice from 18 rides (11%) and placed on two more (22% total)
- Jockey Ryan Moore has won this twice from 15 rides (13%) and placed on five others (47% total)

Race Five: The Sandringham Stakes 5.00pm

Remove horses from the final declaration list in the following order:

1 Any horse priced larger than 33/1 at the off (100%)
2 Any horse drawn higher than 22 (100%)
3 Any horse rated higher than 107 (100%)
4 Any horse who failed to finish in the first nine last time out (96%)
5 Any horse with a run in the last seven days (96%)
6 Any horse with more than three runs this season (96%)
7 Any horse rated higher than 105 (96%)
8 Any horse who failed to finish in the first seven last time out (92%)

Additional Notes:

- Two horses ran in the Newmarket 1000 Guineas and were then successful here on their next start
- Trainer Michael Bell has won this twice from 10 attempts (20%) and placed with two more 40% total)
- Trainer Ed Dunlop has won this twice from nine tries (22%) and place with two others (44% total)
- Trainer Charlie Fellowes has won this twice from three runners (66%)
- Trainer Richard Hannon has won this twice from 12 attempts (17%)

- Trainer Mark Johnston (now Charlie Johnston) has won this twice from 13 runners (15%) and placed with three others (38% total)
- Jockey Frankie Dettori has won this five times from 20 starts (25%) and placed on five others (50% total)
- Jockey Richard Kingscote has won this twice from 10 tries (20%)
- Jockey Jamie Spencer has won this four times from 16 rides (25%) and placed on six others (63% total)
- Jockey Hayley turner has win this twice from seven mounts (29%)

Race Six: The King Edward VII Stakes (Group Two) 5.35pm

Remove horses from the final declaration list in the following order:

1 Any horse priced larger than 18/1 at the off (100%)
2 Any horse who failed to finish in the first 10 last time out (100%)
3 Any horse without a run in the last 60 days (100%)
4 Any horse rated less than 92 (100%)
5 Any horse not in the first six in the betting at the off (100%)
6 Any horse priced larger than 12/1 at the off (96%)
7 Any horse with more than three starts this season (96%)
8 Any horse rated less than 95 (96%)

Additional Notes:

- Six horses came here after running in the Epsom Derby last time out and were successful
- Four horses came here after running in the Fairway Stakes at Newmarket in May last time out and won here
- Two horses came here after running in the Dante Stakes at York last time out and came home first
- Two horses came here after running in the Classic Trial at Sandown Derby last time out and were successful

- Two horses came here after running in Lingfield Derby Trial and went on to win this
- Trainer John Gosden (now John and Thady Gosden) has won this three times from 21 attempts (14%) and placed with seven others (48% total)
- Trainer Mark Johnston (now Charlie Johnston) has won this three times from12 runners (25%) and placed with two others (42% total)
- Trainer Aidan O'Brien has won this three times from 27 runners (11%), and placed with another nine (44% total)
- Trainer Sir Michael Stoute has won this four times from 18 starters (22%) and placed with five others (50% total)
- Trainer Saeed Bin Suroor has won this twice from nine tries (22%)
- Jockey William Buick has won this four times from 10 rides (40%) and placed with one other (50% total)
- Jockey Frankie Dettori has won this four times from 15 rides (27%) and placed on two others (40% total)
- Jockey Ryan Moore has won this three times from 15 mounts (20%) and placed on four others (47% total)
- Jockey Jamie Spencer has won this twice nine rides (22%)

Race Seven: The Palace Of Holyroodhouse Stakes 6.10pm

This race was added in 2020 and therefore we do not have enough statistics to work with

Day Five
Saturday 24th June 2023 (race times and titles subject to change)

Race One: The Chesham Stakes (Listed) 2.30pm

R<u>emove</u> horses from the final declaration list in the following order:

1 Any horse priced larger than 40/1 at the off (100%)
2 Any horse who has raced before but has not been seen on the track in the last 60 days (100%)
3 Any horse who has had more than two races (100%)
4 Any horse who failed to finish in the first five last time out (100%)
5 Any horse who ran in the last seven days (100%)
6 Any horse priced larger than 25/1 at the off (96%)
7 Any horse racing from a stall higher than 12 (96%)
8 Any horse who failed to finish in the first four last time out (96%)
9 Any horse who failed to finish in the first three last time out (92%)
10 Any horse not in the first eight in the betting at the off (92%)

Additional Notes:

- Trainer Paul Cole (now Paul and Oliver Cole) has won this twice from 13 runners (15%) and placed with four others (46% total)
- Trainer John Gosden (now John and Thady Gosden) has won this twice from 12 attempts (17%) and placed with three others (42% total)
- Trainer Mark Johnston (now Charlie Johnston) has won this three times from 32 runners (9%) and placed with six others (28% total)
- Trainer Aidan O'Brien has won this six times from 27 runners (22%) and placed with eight others (52% total)
- Jockey Frankie Dettori has won this four times from 16 rides (25%) and placed on a further two (38% total)
- Jockey Ryan Moore has won this five times from 14 mounts (36%) and placed on three others (57% total)

Race Two: The Jersey Stakes (Group Three) 3.05pm

Remove horses from the final declaration list in the following order:

1 Any horse priced larger than 33/1 at the off (100%)
2 Any horse racing from a stall higher than 20 (100%)
3 Any horse racing from stall one to three (100%)
4 Any horse who failed to finish in the first 11 last time out (100%)
5 Any horse not in the first 10 in the betting at the off (100%)
6 Any horse with an official rating lower than 85 (100%)
7 Any horse priced larger than 25/1 at the off (96%)
8 Any horse with an official rating of less than 93 (96%)
9 Any horse not in the first eight in the betting at the off (96%)
10 Any horse with a rating of less than 100 (92%)
11 Any horse with more than three runs this season (92%)

Additional Notes:

- Five horses came here to win after having their last start in the King Charles II Stakes at Newmarket
- Four horses arrived here after racing in the Newmarket 2000 Guineas and won

~ 67 ~

- Three horses came here from the Irish 2000 Guineas and were successful
- Two horses came here from the Carnarvon Stakes at Newbury and took first place
- Two horses had their last start in the Heron Stakes at Goodwood before winning this
- Trainer Charlie Appleby has won this twice from six runners (33%) and placed with two others (67% total)
- Trainer Richard Fahey has won this twice from seven attempts (29%)
- Trainer Aidan O'Brien has won this three times from 29 runners (10%) and placed with four others (24% total)
- Trainer Sir Michael Stoute has won this three times from 12 runners (25%) and placed with another five (67% total)
- Jockey William Buick has won this twice from 12 rides (17%) and placed on one more (25% total)
- Jockey Jim Crowley has won this twice from nine mounts (22%)

Race Three: The Hardwicke Stakes (Group Two) 3.40pm

Remove horses from the final declaration list in the following order:

1 Any horse priced larger than 14/1 at the off (100%)
2 Any horse drawn higher than 11 (100%)
3 Any horse making their debut (100%)
4 Any horse who failed to finish in the first six last time out (100%)
5 Any horse aged older than six (100%)
6 Any horse outside the first six in the betting at the off (100%)
7 Any horse rated lower than 109 (100%)
8 Any horse who raced in the last seven days (100%)
9 Any horse rated lower than 111 (96%)
10 Any horse with more than three runs this season (96%)

Additional Notes:

- Nine horses came here and won this race after last competing in the Coronation Cup at Epsom
- Three horses came here after running in the Huxley Stakes at Chester and were successful
- Two horses came to win this after running in the Ormonde Stakes at Chester on their last previous start

- Two horses arrived after racing in the Aston Park Stakes at Newbury and went on to win this
- Two winners had their last start in the Brigadier Gerard Stakes at Sandown
- Trainer John Gosden (now John and Thady Gosden) has won this twice from 12 attempts (17%) and placed with three others (42% total)
- Trainer Mark Johnston (now Charlie Johnston) has won this four times from 19 runners (21%) and placed with four others (42% total)
- Trainer Aidan O'Brien has won this four times from 16 attempts (25%) and placed with three others (44% total)
- Trainer Sir Michael Stoute has won this eight times from 36 runners (22%) and placed with eight others (44% total)
- Trainer Saeed Bin Suroor has won this twice from 20 tries (10%) and placed with two others (20% total)
- Jockey Frankie Dettori has won this twice from 13 rides (15%) and placed on five others (54% total)
- Jockey Ryan Moore has won this six times from 15 rides (40%) and placed on one other (47% total)
- Jockey Olivier Peslier has won this three times from five mounts (60%) and placed on one other (80% total)

Race Four: The Queen Elizabeth II Jubilee Stakes (Group One) 4.20pm

Remove horses from the final declaration list in the following order:

1 Any horse priced larger than 33/1 at the off (100%)
2 Any horse drawn in the one stall (100%)
3 Any horse drawn higher than 21 (100%)
4 Any horse aged older than seven (100%)
5 Any horse rated lower than 107 (100%)
6 Any horse returning from 365 days or more off the track (100%)
7 Any horse who finished outside the first 14 last time out (100%)
8 Any horse who finished outside the first 13 last time out (96%)
9 Any horse who finished outside the first 11 last time out (92%)
10 Any horse aged older than six (92%)
11 Any three-year-old (92%)
12 Any horse outside the first 11 in the betting (92%)

Additional Notes:

- Seven horses came here and won after having their previous start in the Duke Of York Stakes at York

~ 71 ~

- Five horses came here and won after racing in the Kings Stand Stakes earlier in the meeting
- Three horses came here and won after last running in the Leisure Stakes at Windsor
- Two horses won this contest after last being seen in the Greenlands Stakes at The Curragh
- Trainer Charlie Appleby has won this twice from five runners (40%) and placed with one other (60% total)
- Trainer James Fanshawe has won this twice from 12 attempts (17%) and placed with three others (42% total)
- Trainer Aidan O'Brien has won this twice from 20 runners (10%) and placed with three others (25% total)
- Jockey James Doyle has ridden in this race seven times and won twice (29%)
- Jockey Ryan Moore has won this three times from 17 rides (18%) and placed on four others (41% total)
- Jockey Tom Queally has won this twice from seven rides (29%)

Race Five: The Wokingham Stakes 5.00pm

Remove horses from the final declaration list in the following order:

1 Any horse priced larger than 33/1 at the off (100%)
2 Any horse making their debut (100%)
3 Any horse aged older than eight (100%)
4 Any horse with more than four runs this season (100%)
5 Any horse rated lower than 87 (100%)
6 Any horse who failed to finish in the first 13 last time out (96%)
7 Any horse aged older than seven (96%)
8 Any horse who failed to finish in the first eight last time out (92%)
9 Any horse rated lower than 91 (92%)
10 Any horse aged older than six (92%)
11 Any horse who failed to finish in the first six last time out (88%)
12 Any horse rated lower than 94 (88%)

Additional Notes:

- Three horses came here after running in the Victoria Cup here in May and went on to be successful
- Three horses last ran in the six-furlong handicap at the Epsom Derby Festival and went on to take this

- Two horses last ran in the six-furlong Class Two handicap at York in May and went on to take this
- Trainer David Evans has won this twice from three runners (67%)
- Trainer Kevin Ryan has won this twice from 28 attempts (7%) and placed with four others (14% total)
- Jockey Ryan Moore has win this twice from 19 rides (11%) and placed on four others (32% total)

Race Six: The Golden Gate Stakes 5.35pm

With only three runnings of this race I cannot provide any worthwhile statistical analysis

Race Seven: The Queen Alexandra Stakes 6.10pm

Remove horses from the final declaration list in the following order:

1 Any horse priced larger than 25/1 at the off (100%)
2 Any horse making their debut on the Flat (100%)
3 Any horse outside the first nine in the betting (100%)
4 Any horse who failed to finish in the first 16 last time out (100%)
5 Any horse rated lower than 87 (100%)
6 Any horse with more than four runs this season (100%)
7 Any horse without a run in the last 365 days (100%)
8 Any horse priced larger than 12/1 at the off (96%)
9 Any horse drawn higher than 16 (96%)
10 Any horse outside the first seven in the betting (96%)
11 Any horse aged older than nine (96%)
12 Any horse without a run in the last 120 days (96%)
13 Any horse outside the first six in the betting (92%)
14 Any horse with more than three runs this season (92%)
15 Any horse rated lower than 92 (92%)

Additional Notes:

- Four horses came here after running in the Ascot Stakes here and were successful
- Four horses came here and won after last racing in the Chester Cup

- Two horses arrived here straight from the Henry II Stakes at Sandown and took first prize
- Two horses last rain in the Aston Park Stakes at Newbury and then won this contest
- Trainer Andrew Balding has won this twice from 10 attempts (20%) and placed with one other (30% total)
- Trainer Gordon Elliott has won this twice from three runners (67%) and placed with the other one (100% total)
- Trainer Mark Johnston (now Charlie Johnston) has won this twice from nine runners (22%) and placed with three others (56% total)
- Trainer Willie Mullins has won this four times from 15 runners (27%) and placed with four others (53% total)
- Trainer Sir Michael Stoute has won this twice from five attempts (40%) and placed with three others (100%)
- Jockey Joe Fanning has won this twice from eight rides (25%) and placed on another two (50% total)
- Jockey Ryan Moore has won this four times from 16 rides (25%) and placed on four others (50% total0
- Jockey Jamie Spencer has won this twice from 14 mounts (14%) and placed on another two (29% total)

Testimonials

Sean and I have worked together for many years now, and his knowledge of racing is well known and respected throughout the industry. If the articles and opinion shared with readers of News - The World of Sport are any indication as to just how valuable this book will be to punters, then it's a "must have" weapon in your punting arsenal. If you do not bet using stats, you will lose more often than you win and, whether you bet for profit or fun, you need this on your side"

Ron Robinson – Owner, The World of Sport

"Sean Trivass is better known as the 'Statman' to my readers and has contributed excellent comprehensive articles on horse racing for my monthly newsletter What really Wins Money. His stats angles are totally unique and a real deep dive into the world of horse racing stats based betting angles.

He's looked at jockeys, trainers, race courses, sires and dams (breeding), the draw, the all weather, favourites, 2nd and 3rd favourites , ground conditions, race distance, handicaps versus non-handicap and many other angles, for both the horse racing backer and layer.

There have been some real eye-catching finds from Sean's work, some of which I use myself. This guy knows his onions! "

Clive Keeling – What Really Wins Money

"Statistics can be presented in many a varied manner for varied reasons and we are right to retain a sceptical mind of them and how *and why they are revealed. However, with horse racing they are a vital component and my colleague Sean Trivass is an equally vital component in collating and interpreting them for our use.*

Watching, listening, reading Sean's dissection of a field using his calibrated statistics is a racing marvel. He professes to not liking full-sized handicap fields, but in reality he is in his element pouring over the variables using his statistics as he slices and dices the field into a logical order for the likes of you and I to understand.

Group 1 elite contests to the full field handicaps are all part of Sean's vision and depth of years of experience. From watching the world's best on the track to a humble maiden, he approaches each contest with the same enthusiasm to find the outcome

I have watched and enjoyed Sean's work for twenty years as we have travelled to race meetings in many parts of the globe and when back home in Australia he is my guide for UK racing. Racing is international, broadcasting 24 hours a day somewhere in the world, and Sean's delving into the statistics give us all a steady platform to participate".

Rob Burnet
Editor
Thoroughbrednews.com.au

Finally, should you have any questions (no abuse thank you, all of this has been written in good faith) or just want to know a little bit more about my upcoming projects and books, feel free to contact me via *www.writesports.net*

Printed in Great Britain
by Amazon